Introduction

Louis Thomas Jérôme Auzoux (1797–1880), a French doctor and naturalist, invented anatomical (and botanical) papier-mâché models that were widely distributed in the 19th and 20th centuries. Historians date the project to launch his own production factory to a visit to the papier-mâché workshop of Jean-François Ameline in 1820. Apparently the former medical student recalled the frustrating lack of human remains available for dissection purposes for the study of anatomy, and so conceived of a technical and commercial process called “anatomy clastic” (from the Greek *klastos*, broken in pieces), consisting of complex models with detachable parts, enabling the body’s general structure as well as internal organs to be revealed. The use of papier-mâché instead of wax allowed costs to be considerably reduced, and guaranteed greater resistance to frequent handling. Located in Saint-Aubin-d’Écrosville, Auzoux’s Normandy hometown, the Maison Auzoux enjoyed a moment of glory and distributed its models not only to hospitals, but also to universities and schools. Its creations can now be found in science museums, in the hands of antique dealers, and at specialized auctions.

This book presents a series of works by John Armleder based on these models, which he acquired partly by accident, and somewhat mischievously. In the interview with Mai-Thu Perret which follows, we come to understand that it is not so much the educational or iconographical dimension of these objects that the artist wished to reproduce, but rather the cascade of references to questions, technical as much as abstract or material, and also linked to figuration. Armleder therefore addresses questions of reproduction, displacement, and meaning, always in their multiple shifts, contradictions, and bifurcations.

—Lionel Bovier

John Armleder
Out! (Out!)

jrp|ringier

To Martin Hansen

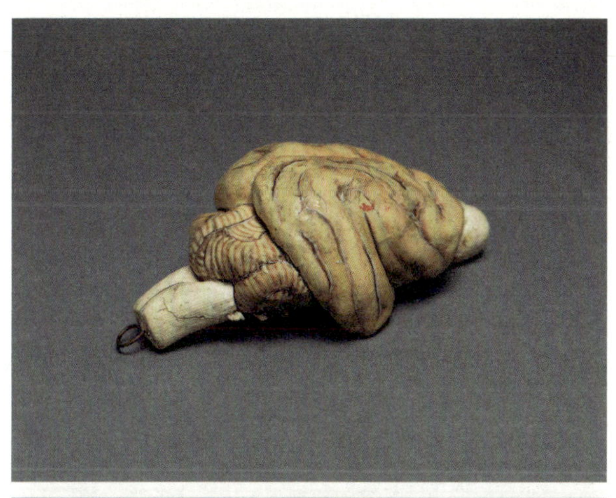

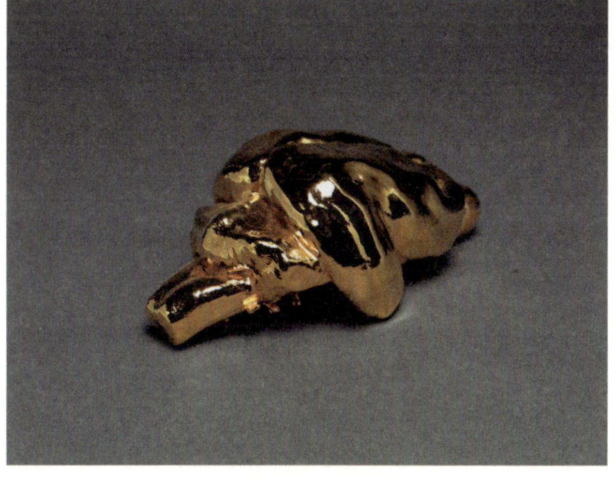

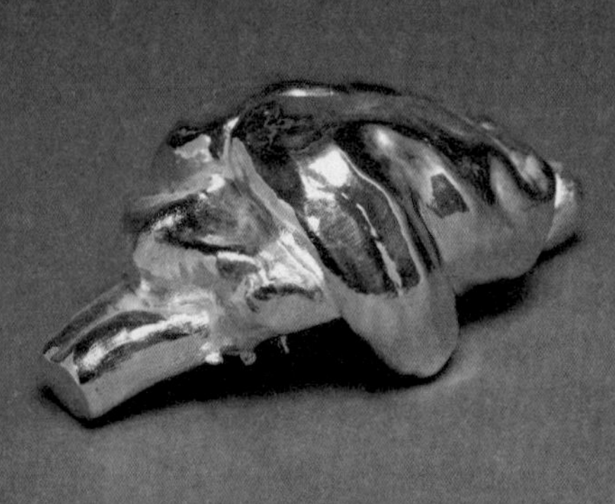

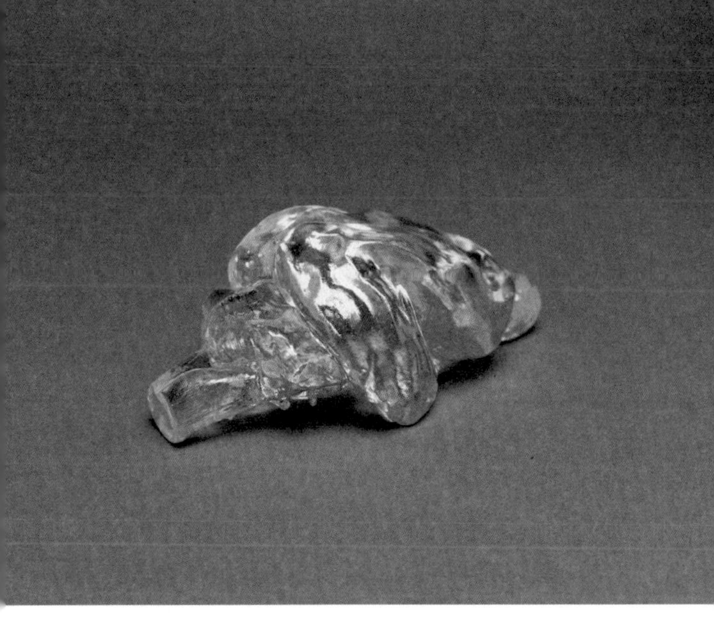

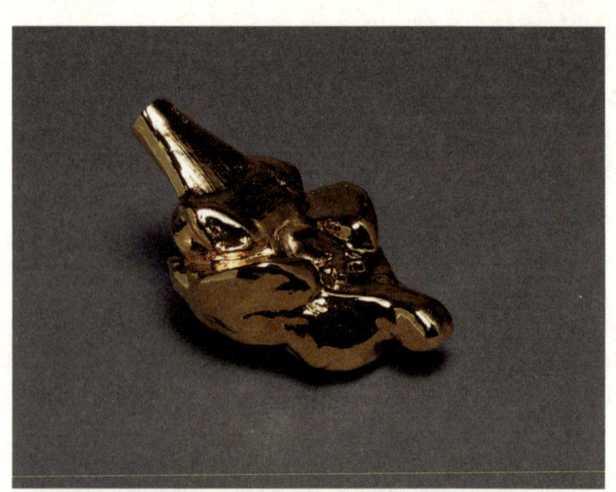

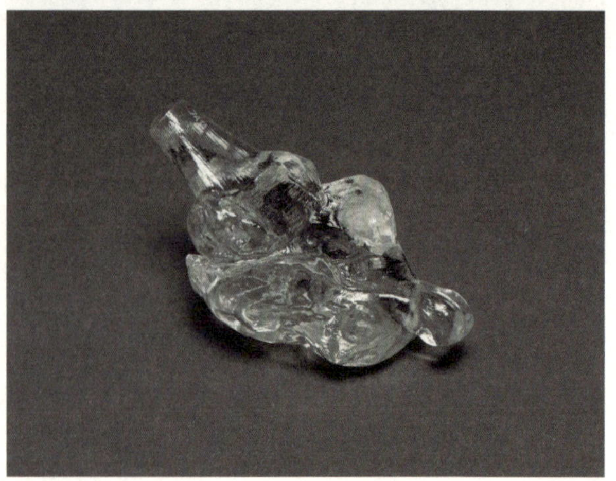

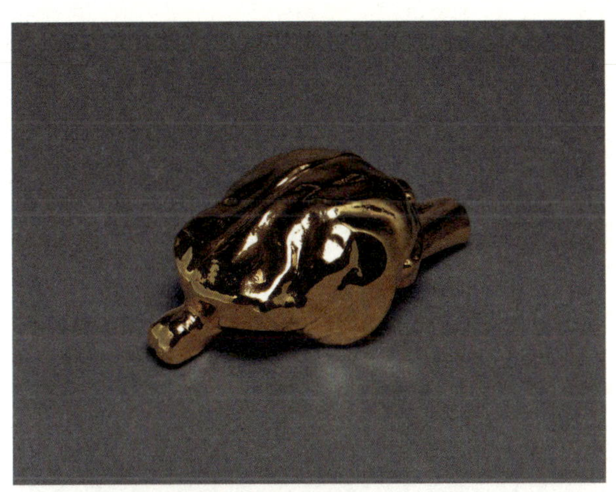

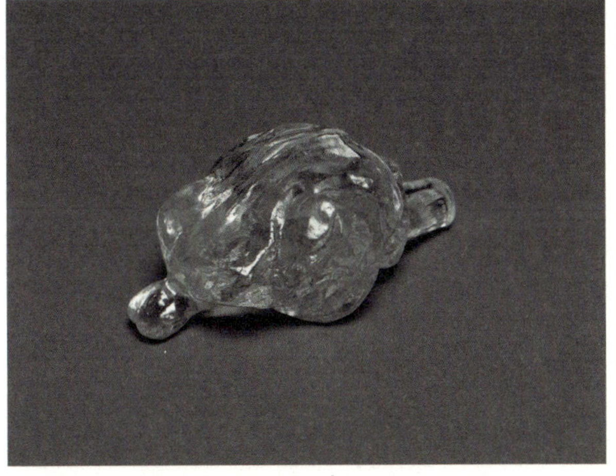

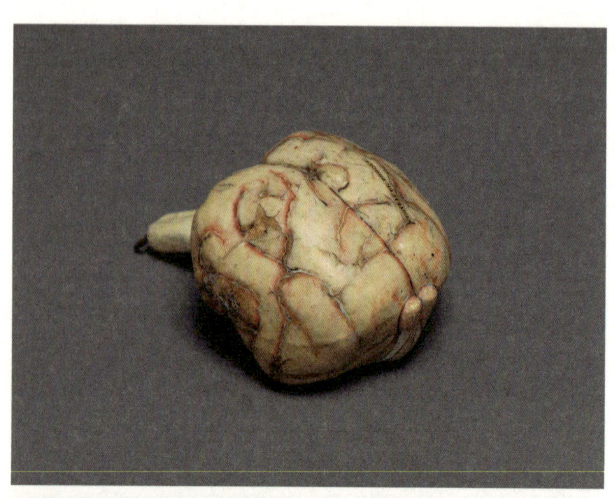

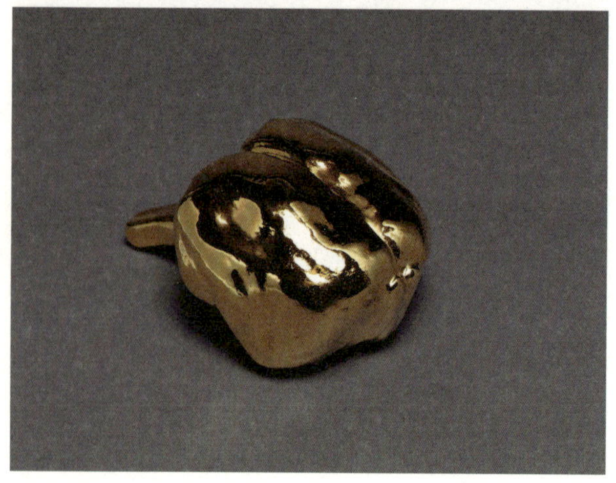

False Leads

A Conversation between John Armleder and Mai-Thu Perret

MTP – The main works in your recent exhibition at the Galerie Andrea Caratsch in Zurich (*Out! (Out!)*, Summer 2015) are versions of brains in different materials. Where exactly did this iconography originate?

JA – It is from a collection of various animal brains modeled by Doctor Auzoux in the mid-19th century. They are made out of papier-mâché on various scales. Doctor Auzoux had developed this process to reproduce anatomical and botanical models. In a completely fortuitous way, during a trip to London, I saw this collection in the window of a fashion store. I asked whether it was for sale and it was, so I purchased the collection.

MTP – These objects show an educational process vis-à-vis science.

JA – Doctor Auzoux began by providing models of human bodies to medical colleges, and then realized that these models could also be useful in schools and could be sold to inform the general public about human and animal anatomy, as well as about botany. At that time it was definitely more complicated and expensive to use other materials than papier-mâché. His idea was to popularize models for educational purposes, to disseminate knowledge so that it could reach the broadest audience: it was a social idea. But it was also an entrepreneur's idea, with the intention of mass-producing these models. Auzoux opened a small factory, but the business went bankrupt and was taken over by someone else, who continued production for a few years, until it was abandoned altogether. I believe similar experiments were undertaken in other countries, in particular in Germany, during this period. In a certain way, it was a phase in the history of the dissemination of knowledge inaugurated in the 19th century by figures such as Ernst Haeckel and, in a less democratic form, Leopold and Rudolf Blaschka with their famous models in glass and Bohemian crystal.

MTP – Can you describe what you decided to do with these models originally destined for scientific purposes? The original objects have now become items for modern cabinets of curiosities, as well as decorative objects.

JA – Of course, there is a kind of drift in perception and use. These objects are now collected as curios and not as objects of learning, even though they are still sometimes used in certain schools. Although it was ironic to find them in a fashion store, I've clearly emphasized their semantic shift of meaning by making use of them as models: the paper objects, conceived so as to avoid the wax print, have been cast and produced in several materials totally inappropriate for the dissemination of knowledge, such as silver- or gold-plated bronze, glass, and even fluorescent uranium glass. The fact that someone spent his/their time modeling non-visible elements, such as human anatomy, by creating objects that would then be collected for their symbolic and aesthetic qualities is a kind of shift that interests me.

MTP – These works are therefore reproductions of reproductions of brains realized in relatively precious (or "artistic") materials, such as bronze or glass. Furthermore, they are presented in display cases.

JA – More than a framework, the display cases give an appropriate context to these objects. What interested me, in fact, was using emblematic sculptural techniques to reproduce what was, initially, a simple object of scientific demonstration or of dissemination of knowledge generally. This historical and material misinterpretation generates another interpretation, which is also interesting. If these objects are now collected for their aesthetic value, we can deduce from this that their additional "transfer" into the domain of art, celebrated by a different "value" (whatever it may be), responds to a certain logic.

MTP – Could we say that you start with an educational object or with an object that has a practical purpose, and that you transform it into a fetish object?

JA – In a way that's what we always do with art objects ...

MTP – There are precedents in your work with the brain motif: the mural paintings *Loasaceae* and *Loasaceae Double*, the pair of twin brains in glass and silver that you offered as a multiple, all from 2002.

JA – The brain has been a recurring subject of my work since the beginning of the 1990s, first as a "calligraphic" motif, then as an "object." These works always focus on the human brain,

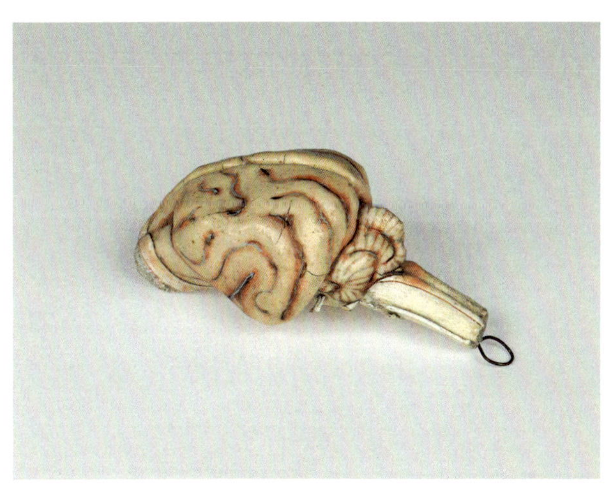

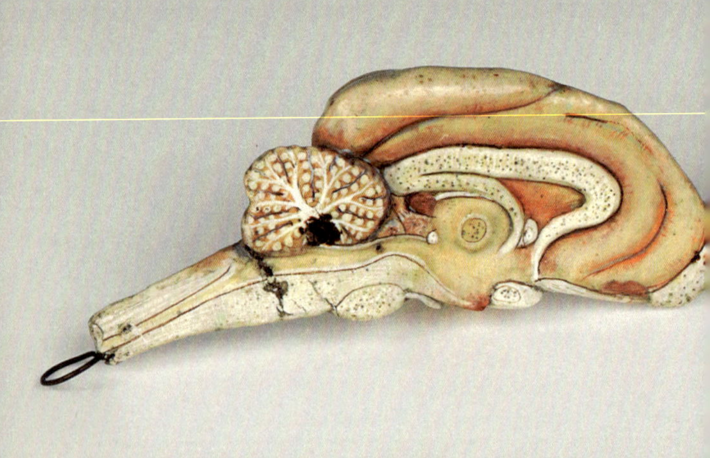

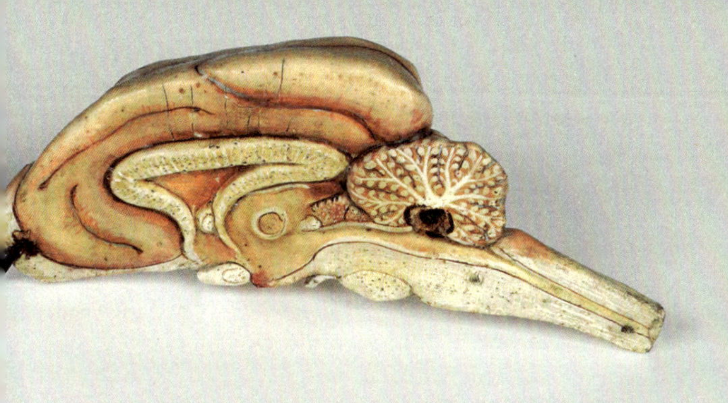

which does not appear in the work we are discussing here (even though the brains of primates and some other animals are very similar). The first brain "object" was modeled on a 1:1 scale; then I made enlarged versions, by testing manufacturing limits, arriving at a model in glass about 1.2 meters long ... A new meaning appeared in this transfer between the idea, motif, and manufacture. I don't exactly know why, but this is what interests me. By taking a formally complete image—as I was able to do previously with the motif of the skull—and by using it either as a motif or as the base object from which to create a sculpture, we diverge from the meaning of the subject without losing its force.

Because I had a health problem related to my brain several years ago, when people now look at these works, they easily apply a biographical interpretation to them, even though my work is not autobiographical.

MTP – These objects are fascinating because they participate in this desire—inherited from the Enlightenment—for knowledge about the body's interior, including the desire to expose all that is hidden. We are at a crossroads of science and human desire, because these models have practical reasons for existing (for example, the lack of cadavers for dissection, the cost of

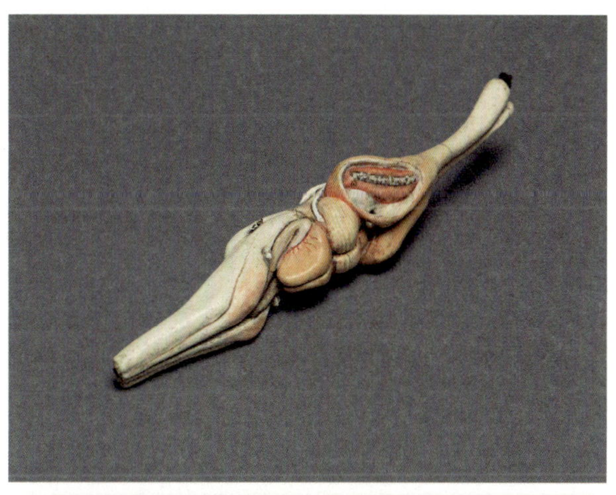

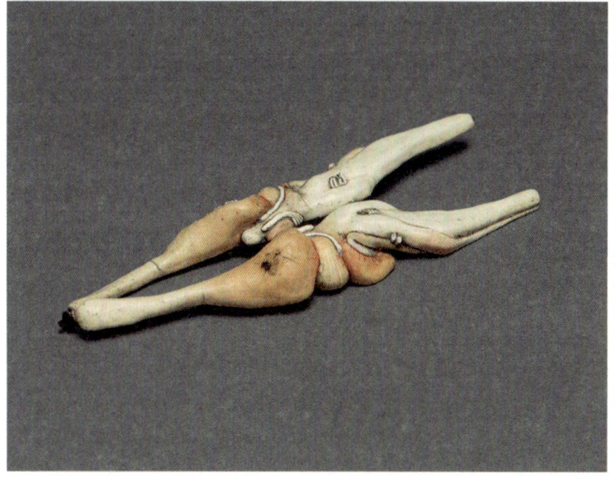

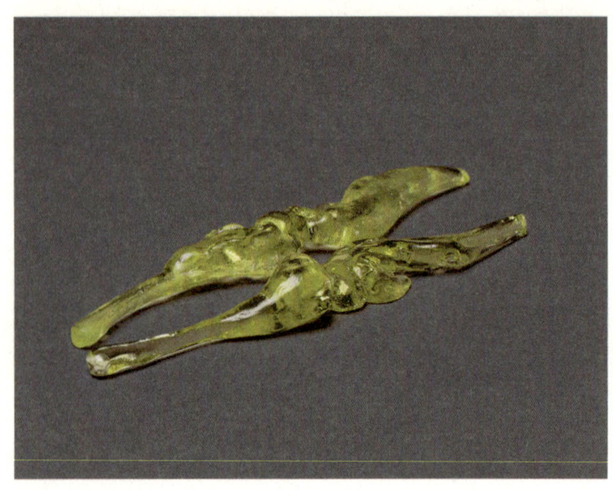

the first replicas of human anatomy) and they are also products of a period when the absence of religious impediments invited openness ...

JA – Yes, there is a whole parallel narrative that this artwork's manufacture is not really concerned with. What interests me is the complex geometry of these objects, which we understand are functional, but whose purpose we don't really grasp. In short, it is a leap *to the side* of the idea of pure geometry (the black square, the perfect sphere, the rejection of all ornamentation), and when we reinstitute this motif as ornamentation, as I did with the mural paintings, the meaning is both displayed and irremediably lost.

MTP – Is this also the case with your mural paintings based on protozoan or single-cell animals drawn by Ernst Haeckel?

JA – Haeckel theorized evolution by giving a meaning of perfection to the aesthetic amelioration of the object. It's for this reason that he laid them out on sheets engraved according to aesthetic criteria he considered meaningful.

MTP – The notion that, at the heart of creation (even though it is not a religious creation but a creation based on the theory of evolution), at the heart of living matter or the structure of the world, there was something like a form of beauty.

JA – Exactly. With the corollary that the more something is beautiful, the more it is right, the more it is evolved. My efforts take an opposite direction: they are more focused on the disappearance of the object. From the moment when the object is repeated as a motif or presented as a decorative object, we step away from knowledge, from the aesthetic or the construction of a moral signification.

I am aware of the ambiguity involved in transforming instruments for making knowledge accessible into art objects, displayed in showcases like collector items. There is an accumulation of false leads. But as soon as we head in one direction, aren't we always following a false lead? Isn't it the multiplication of false leads that can alone eventually lead us to some kind of revelation—not *the* revelation, but a revelation of some sort?

MTP – Your choices don't happen by chance, because they always have a relation to specific objects. This is akin to many other artists' practices. I'm thinking, in particular, of the series of bronze and glass skulls by Sherrie Levine (*Crystal Skull: 1-12*, 2010) inspired by phrenology, a pseudoscience of the 19th century that tried to link the skull's size and morphology directly to evolution and intelligence.

JA – I think that the historically radical gesture of reproduction in the history of art is not very different from that of reusing an image disseminated by knowledge generally ... This is something that probably distances both Sherrie Levine and myself from a practice like that of Mark Dion, which intends to imitate or recreate a scientific element, even if only through its "display."

MTP – There is indeed, in Mark Dion's work, a kind of archeology of knowledge, the determination to be in the position of a scientist—with the specific aesthetic that goes with that. In your case, there is always a kind of detachment: the object is detached from its origin, its discourse, and put into "weightlessness."

JA – Bad reasons rather than good lead to the production of something: the object of knowledge manufactured so that it will be disseminated in a generally accessible way ends up as décor in a fashion store, and, reworked by an

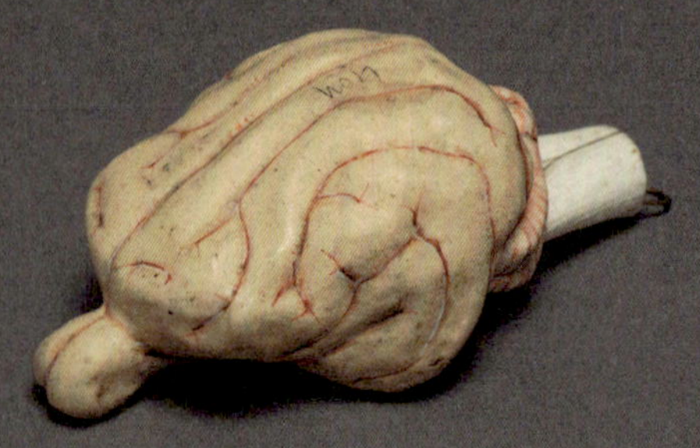

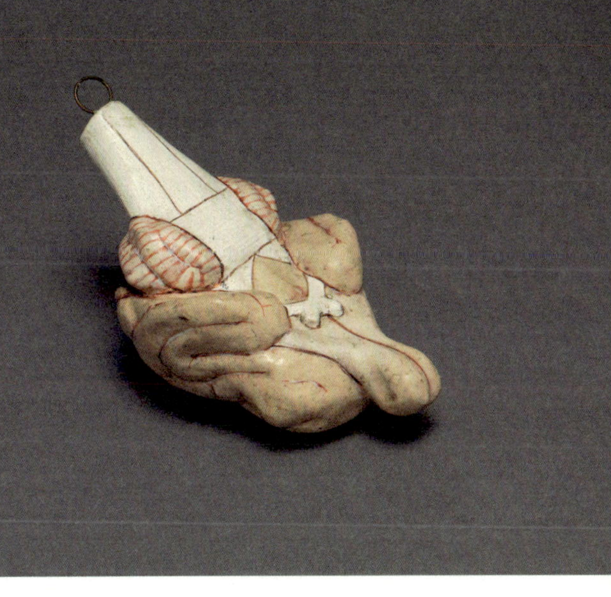

artist, finishes in an art gallery as a "precious" object. It is not really precious like a diamond would be—intrinsically—but because it is taken on by a system in which it is exclusive.

MTP – Looking at Doctor Auzoux's works, I am fascinated by the process of duplication behind the production of these objects. The models of complete human bodies attest to the extraordinary care taken to reproduce the details of such a complex whole, for example, the uteruses illustrating the different stages of a baby's development. Auzoux also explained how he used peritoneum from a bull to line a human interior and show what happens when a hernia develops. There was an extreme refinement to the manufacture of these objects that you erase completely by reproducing them via casting methods: in fact, a large number of the effects of these objects were produced with paint—the veins, for example, are in relief, but also painted. In your work, you abstract these representations, remove colors and, in the end, produce a much more classical sculpture.

JA – I remove the color and I negate the material by producing transparent objects or objects with reflective surfaces. The papier-mâché was originally molded in a relatively complex way, not only in the sense of a manual fabrication, but also in terms of mass production. I do everything the wrong way: I chose heavy, vaguely precious materials, and only produce a few copies. There is a set of adopted misinterpretations. The system of false leads put in place may perhaps indicate something that other people will judge meaningful, but without me having the slightest control over the signposting of said leads.

What is interesting with art is that often the performance or the product is offered without any signposting. One of the reasons for which, after not giving my works titles for many years, I began to do so for cataloguing reasons, is that my titles have strictly nothing to do with the objects themselves: they are selected by chance from lists that do not relate at all to the original object. They are added a posteriori, hence without an attempt at illustration; in brief, they throw out leads, which, if they are not false, are in any case not intentional.

It is possible that the agitation provoked by all these non-meanings, these erroneous meanings, and these false leads produces something. Perhaps not. In the end, it is not important. It is a little Duchampian to affirm this, but another interpretation would be very reductive: being interested in the purely aesthetic or purely scientific quality of such an act of showing would shunt us into a siding and not into a cul-de-sac. There's a big difference!

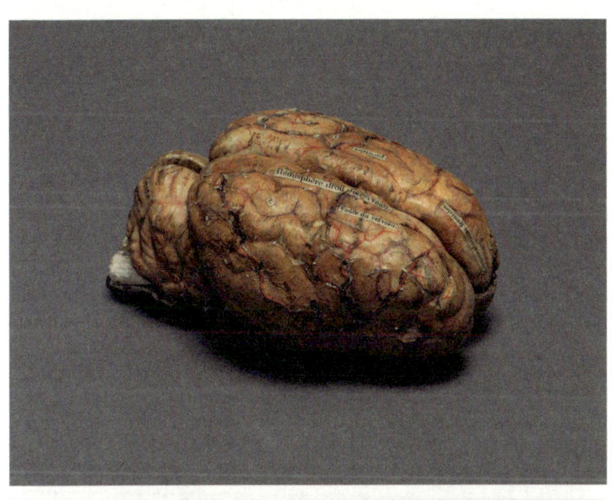
Hémisphère droit
Voûte du cerveau.

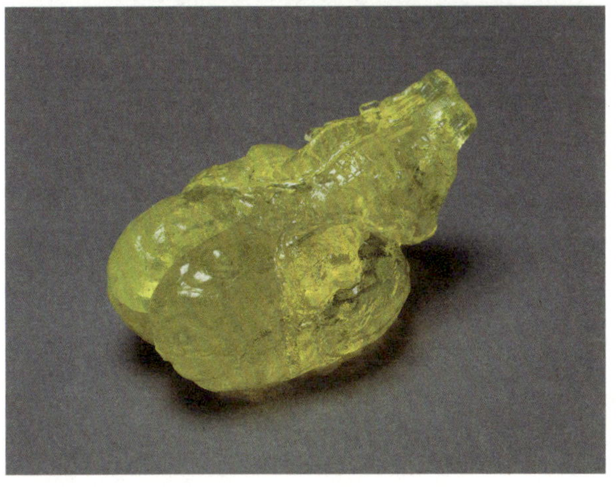

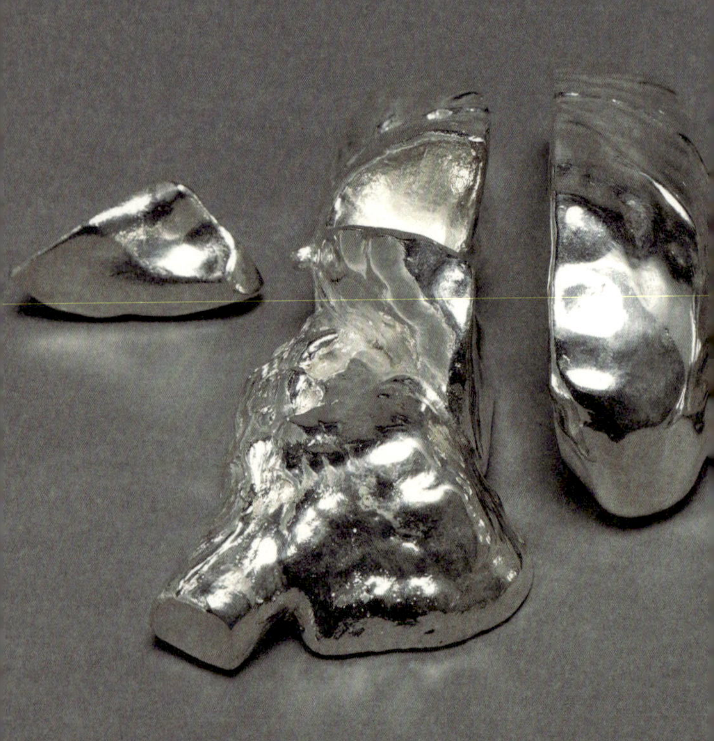

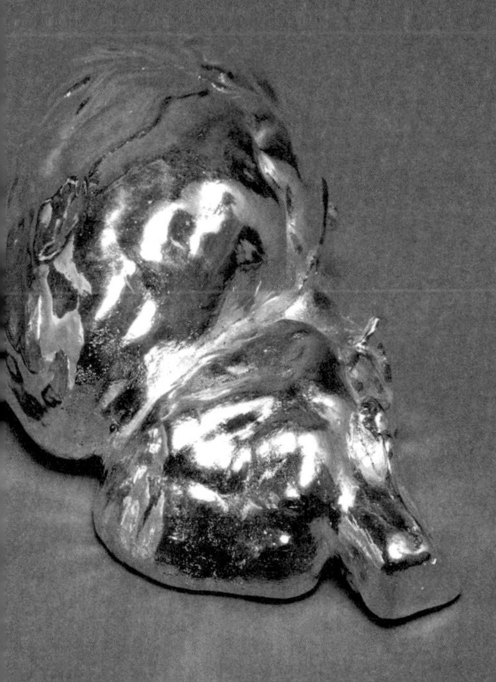

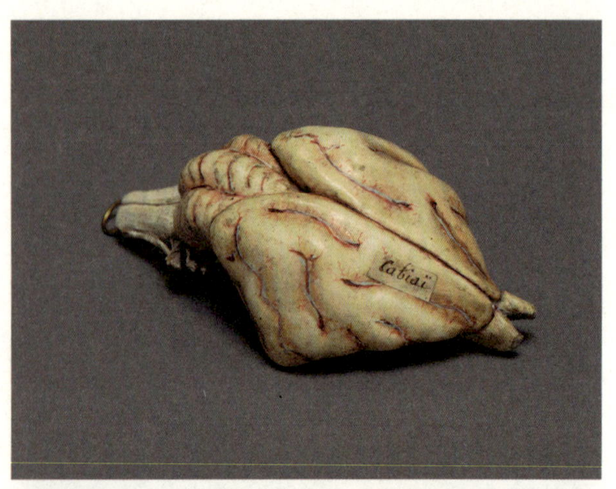
Cabiaï

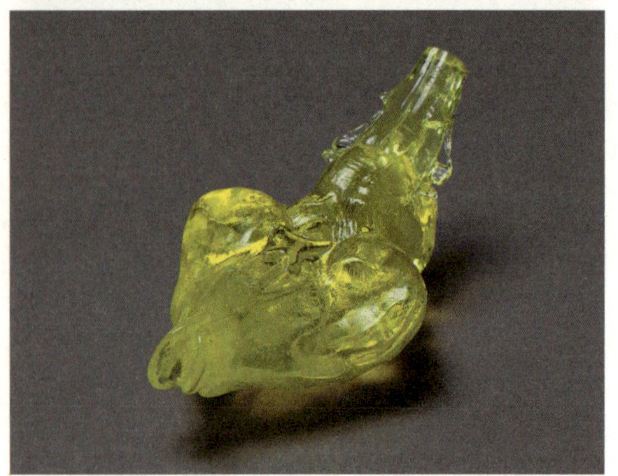

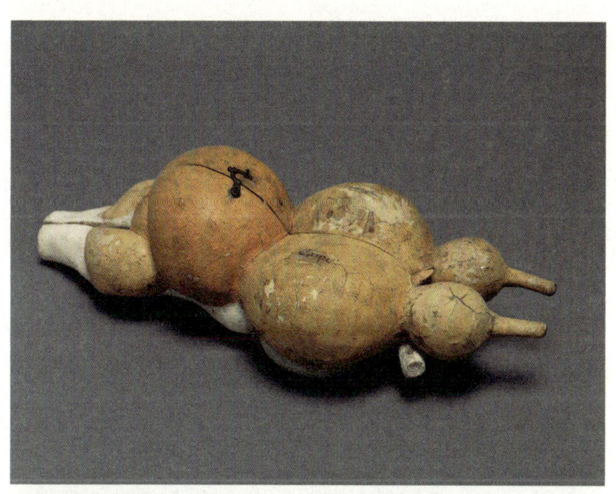

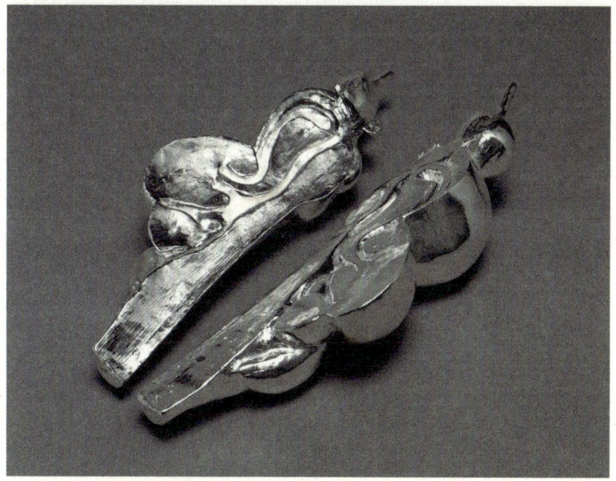

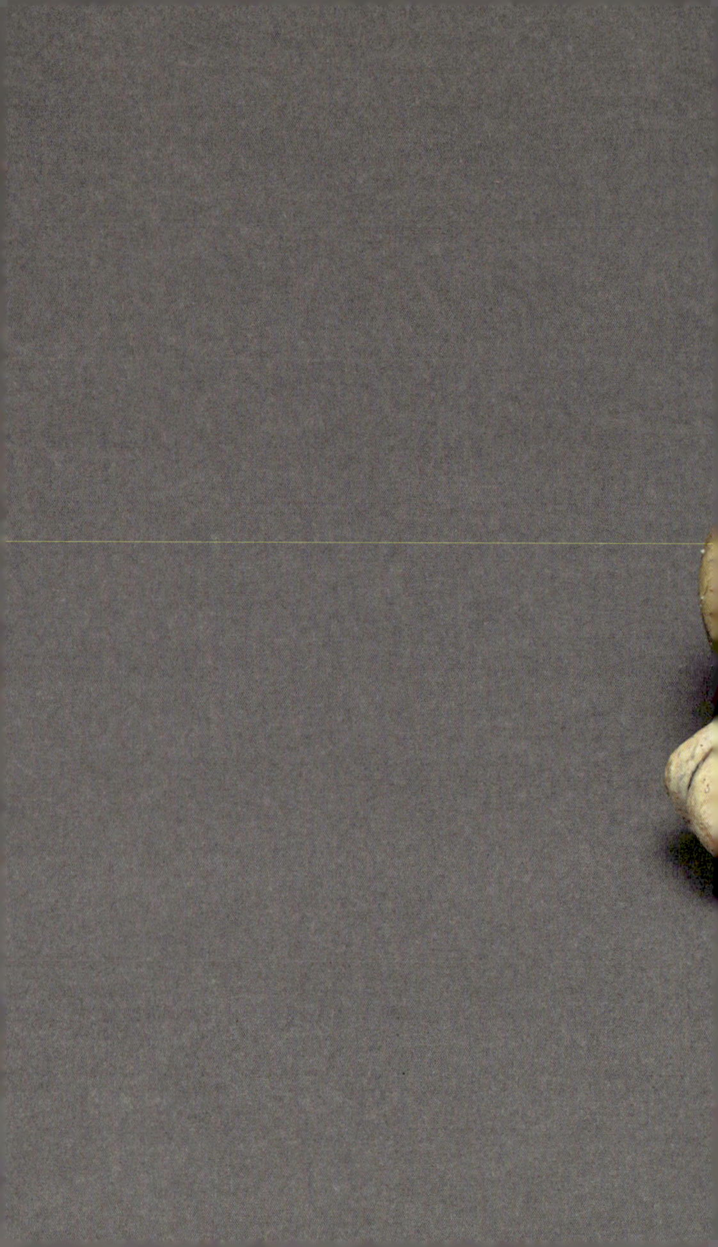

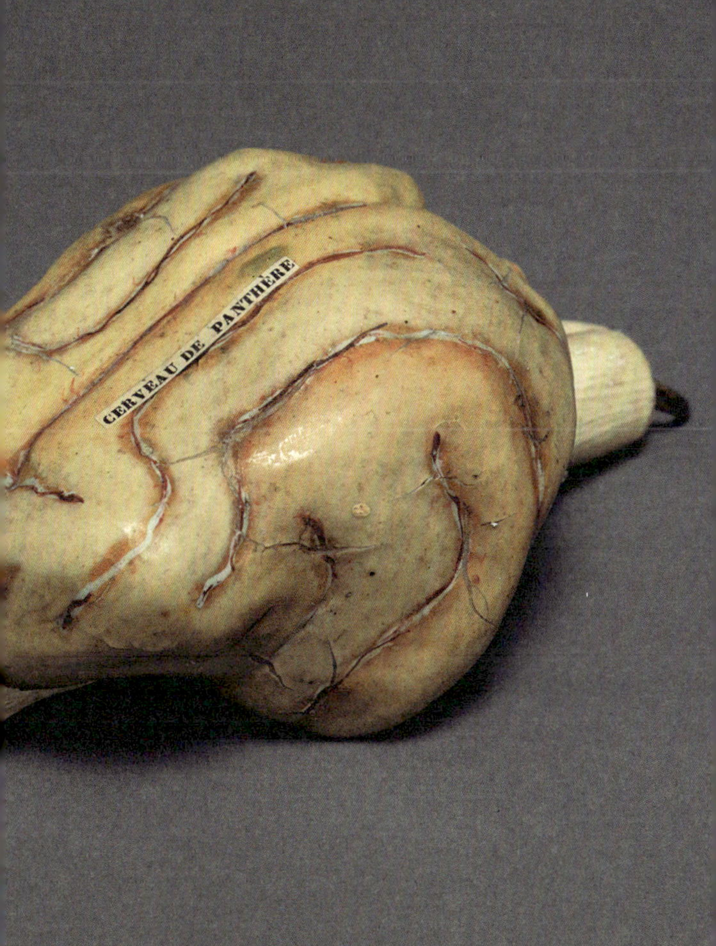
CERVEAU DE PANTHÈRE

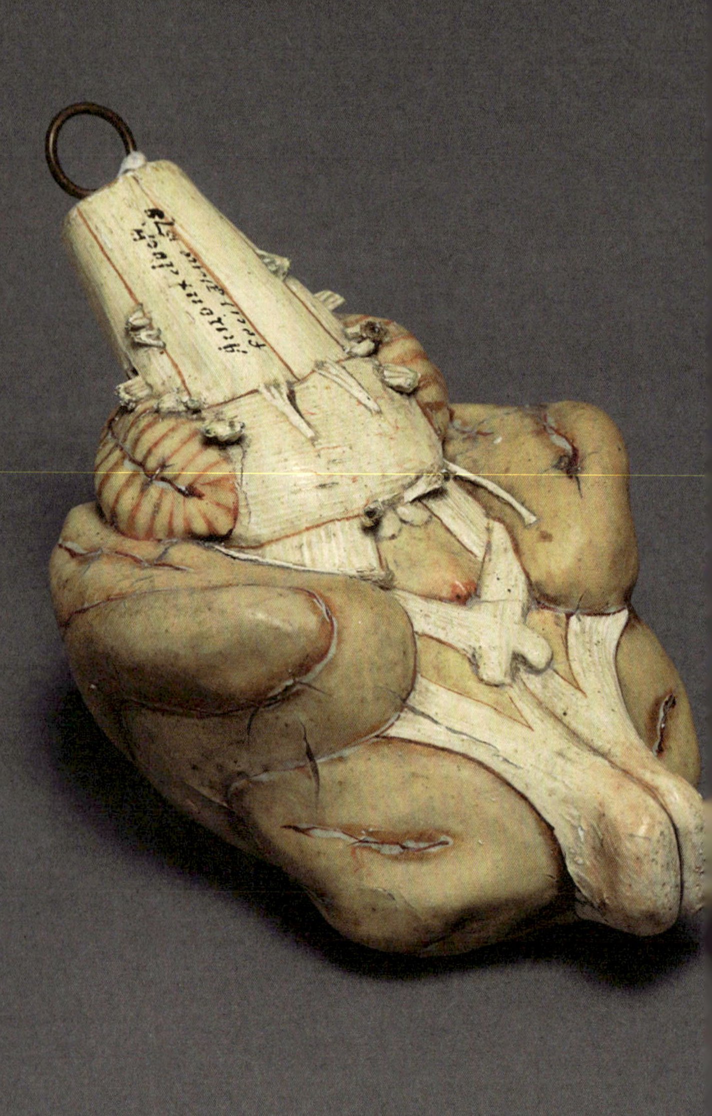

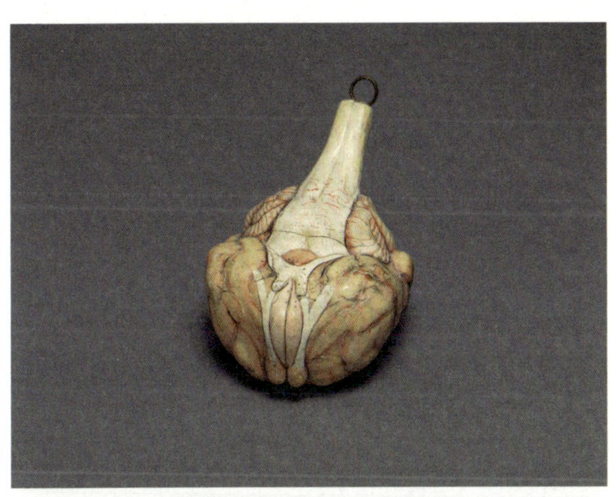

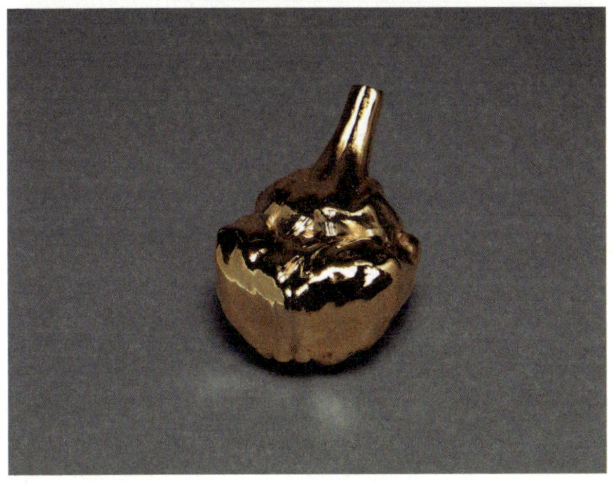

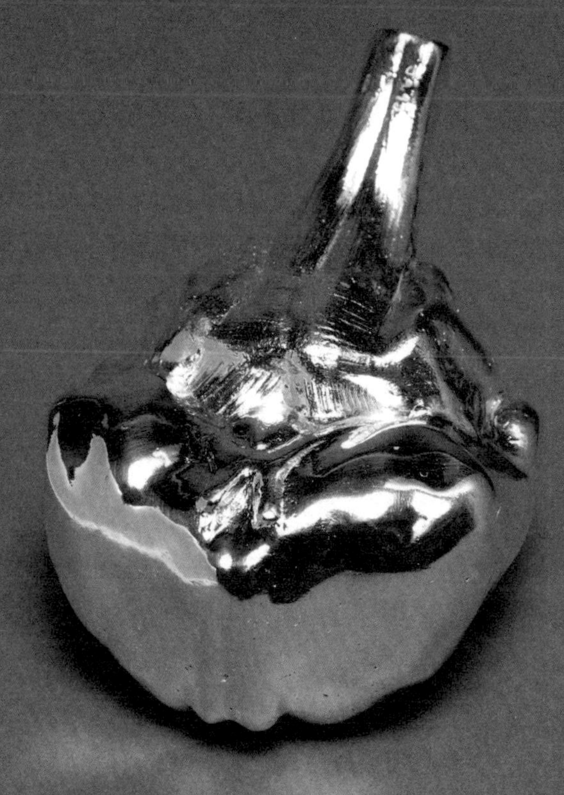

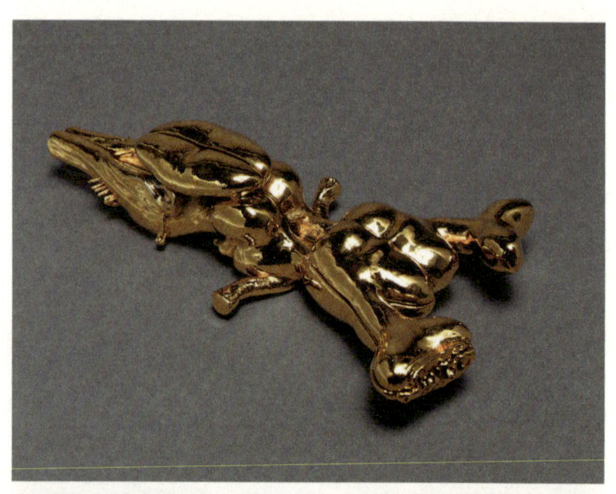

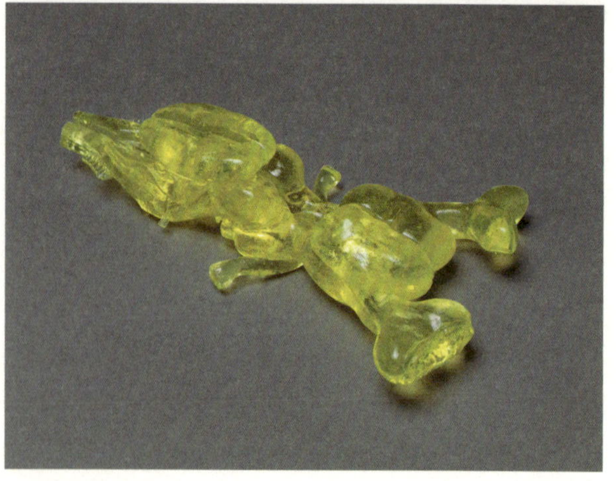

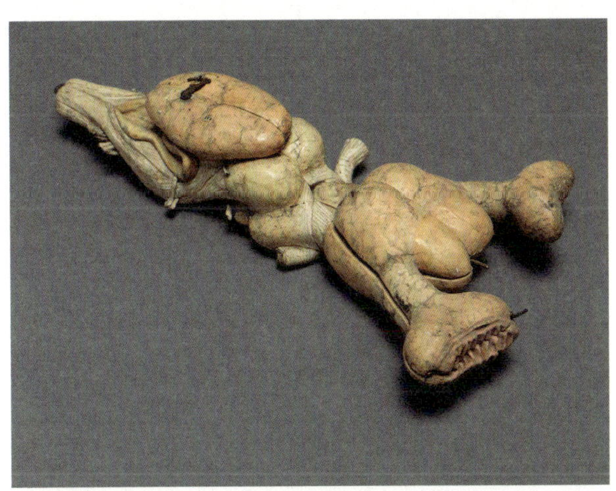

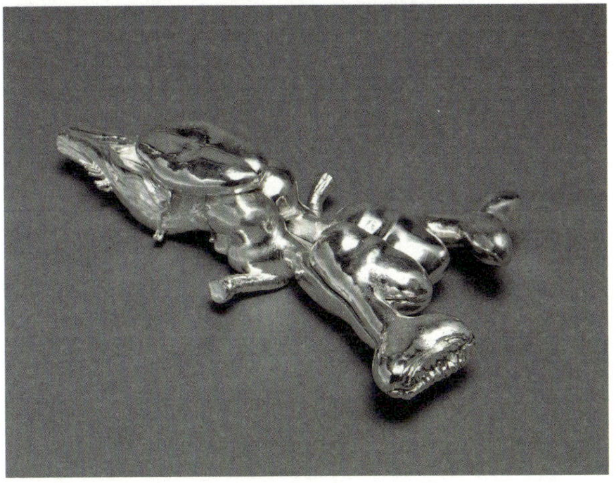

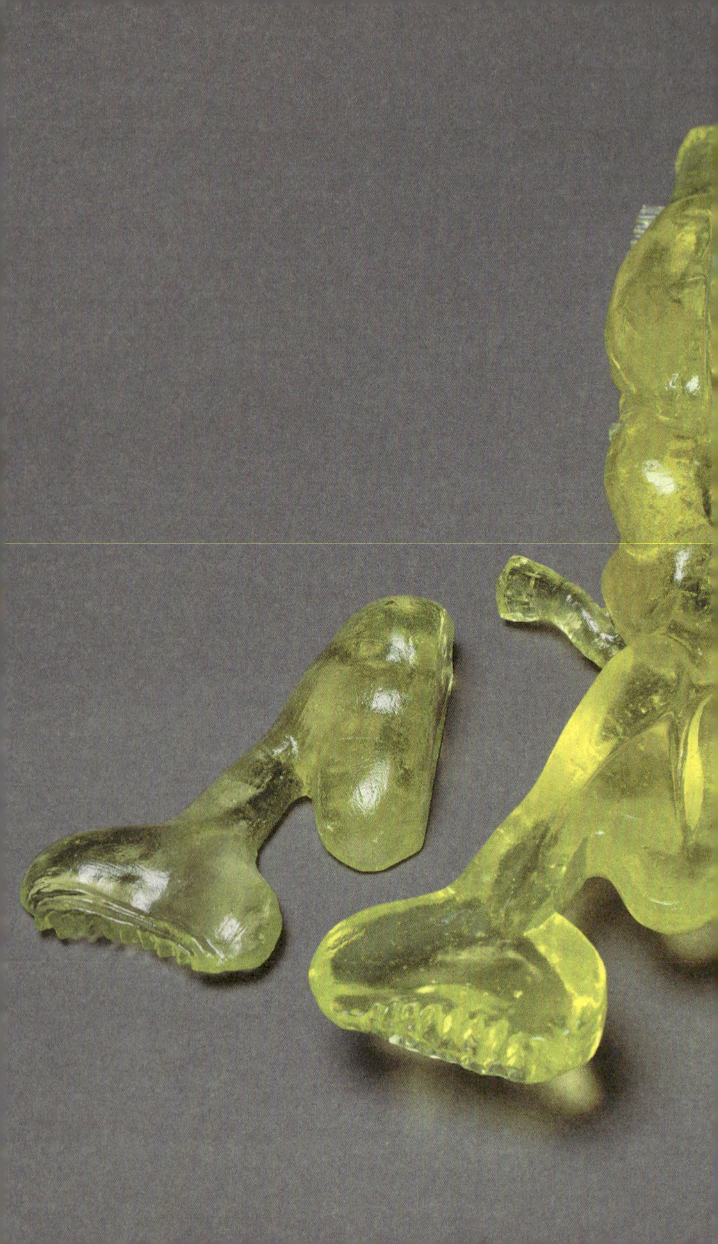

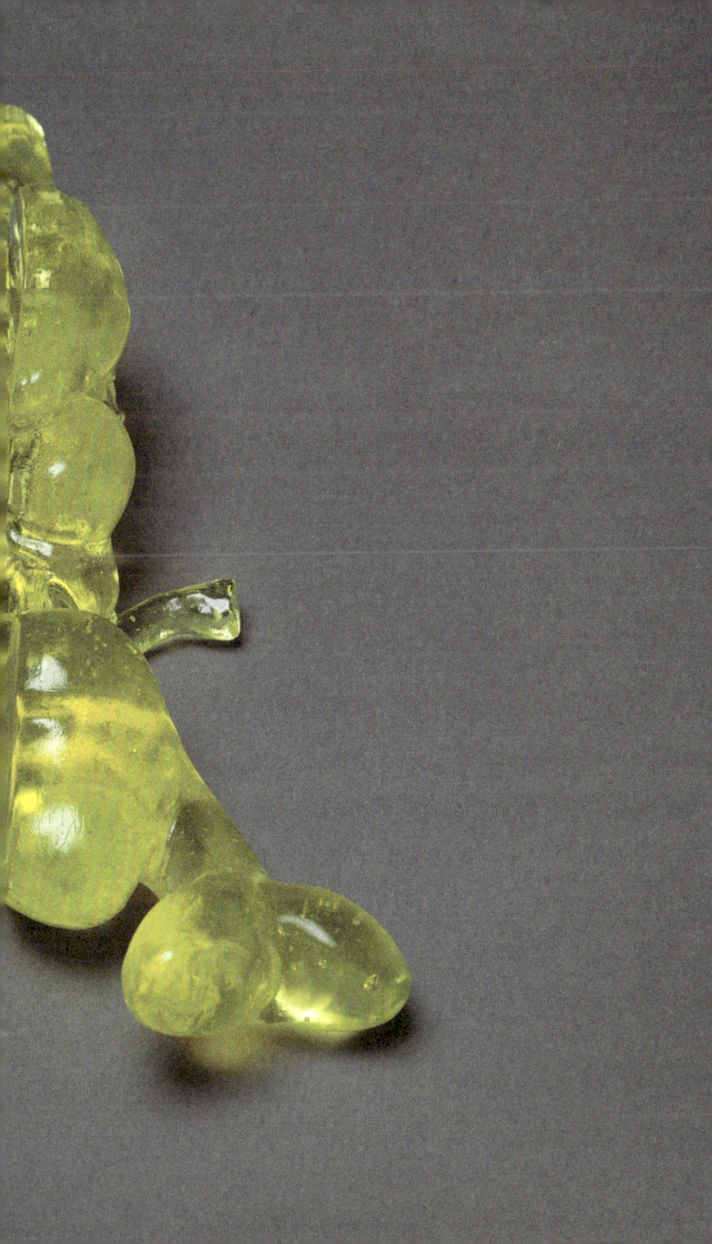

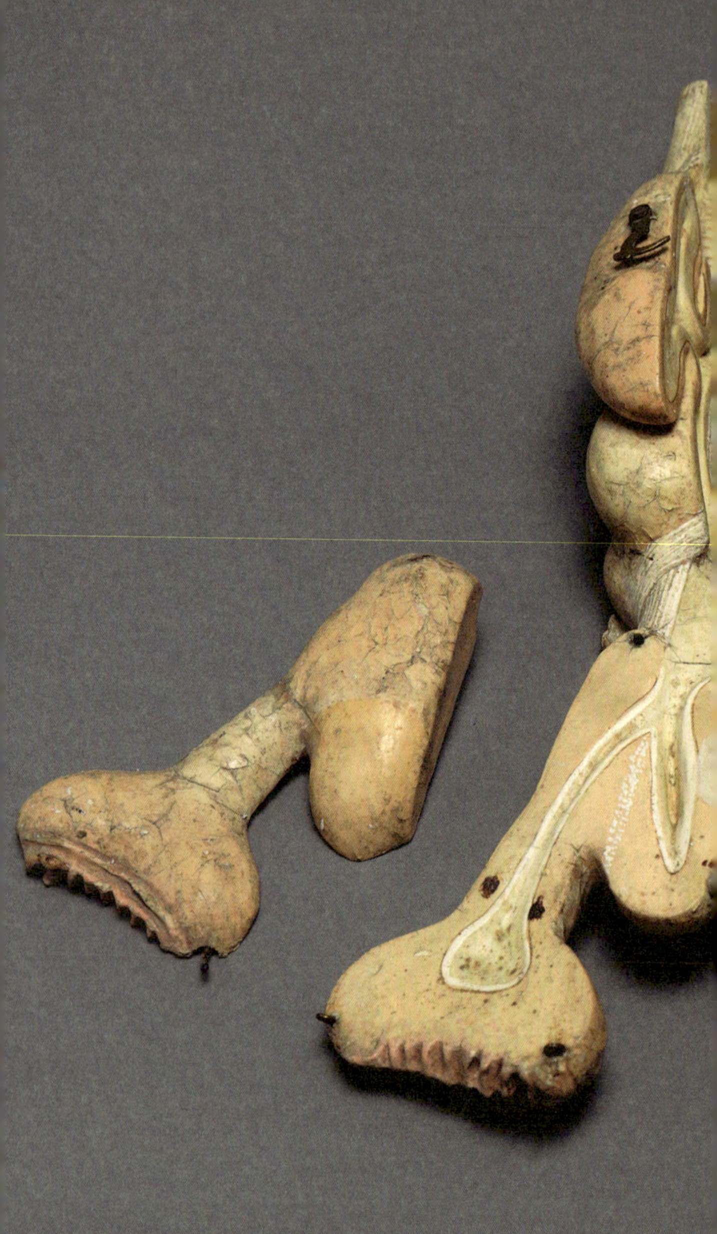

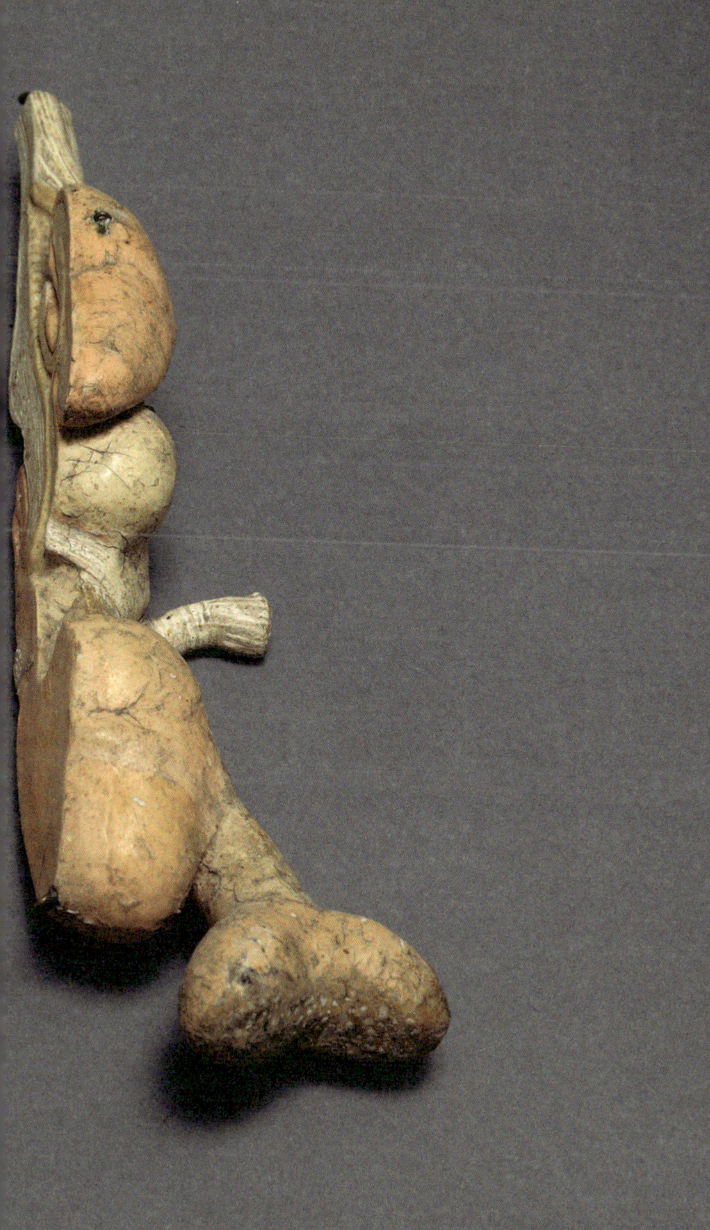

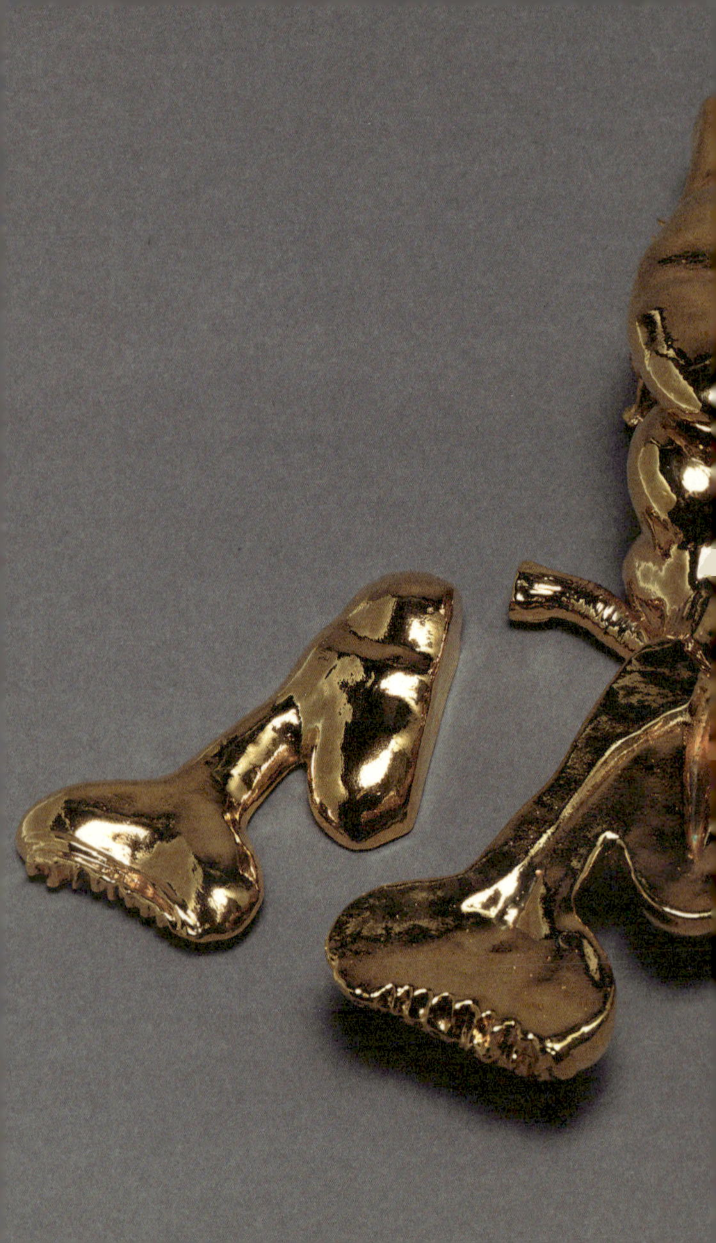